Book of Beginnings and Ends

Also by Christopher Howell

POEMS:

The Grief of a Happy Life
Love's Last Number
Gaze
Dreamless and Possible: poems New & Selected
Light's Ladder
Just Waking
Though Silence: the Ling Wei Texts
Memory and Heaven
Sweet Afton
Sea Change
Why Shouldn't I
The Crime of Luck

ANTHOLOGIES:

Hair of the Dog
Heart of the Rat
Aspects of Robinson: Homage to Weldon Kees (with Christopher Buckley)

LIMITED EDITIONS:

The Bear in the Mirror
Red Alders in an Island Dream
The Wu General Writes from far Away
Lady of the Fallen Air (poems from the Chinese)
King of the Butterflies
The Jetty

Book of Beginnings and Ends

poems

CHRISTOPHER HOWELL

STEPHEN F. AUSTIN STATE UNIVERSITY PRESS

For more information:
Stephen F. Austin State University Press
P.O. Box 13007 SFA Station
Nacogdoches, Texas 75962
sfapress@sfasu.edu
www.sfasu.edu/sfapress
936-468-1078

Distributed by Texas A&M University Press Consortium
www.tamupress.com

Production Manager: Kimberly Verhines
Book Design: Madyson Meares
Cover Art: Ria Harboe: "Pier to the Deep Blue" 15"x13" Acrylic on Panel

CONTENTS

III.
The Godly Sea

I.V.
Come Near Us Again

ACKNOWLEDGMENTS

My thanks to the editors of the following publications in which poems in this volume originally appeared:

The American Journal of Poetry: "Some Wars Never End,"
    "Standing Still," "Summer"
Basalt: "Night Time," "Devotion"
Bellingham Review: "Sartre"
The Birmingham Poetry Review: "The Magician is Surprised to Find
    Nothing in his Hat"
The Cresset: "Relearning to Pray"
Field: "Looking Glass Edge," "Her Sticky Name"
Gettysburg Review: "Noah at Last," "Each Night an Opera House,"
    "Poem for the Turn of the Year," "For Gerald, a Letter,"
    "Waking I do not Wish Life to Leave Me Soon," "Night
    Caller," "The Four Directions"
Glassworks: "Memory's House"
Hotel Amerika: "The End of the Affair"
I-70 Review: "Lamont Cranston in Retirement," "Old Beginnings
    and Ends," "Semaphore upon the Matter of Age," "After
    his Dream of the End of the World"
Image: "Friend"
New Letters: "A Messenger," "He Addresses the Inner Life"
Orion: "The Old Farmers Speak to the New"
Pleiades: "Often I Begin with Nothing"
Plume: "Blue Chair"
Salt: "An Empty Barrel, Listening," "The Seaside,"
    "Bread upon the Waters," "Night Ops"
Sou'wester: "Whisper"
The Swamp: "At the Very End of Summer"
Terminus: "Elegy for Uncle Glen"
Tampa Review: "Not Alice"
Windfall: "Above the Oaks Park Amusement Arcade the Beloved
    Dead Come Near Us Again"

"Flood," appeared in *In Like Company* (MadHat Press, Asheville, North Carolina), 2015.

The author wishes to thank also Melissa Kwasny, David Axelrod, and Christopher Buckley, for their friendship and for their generous and thoughtful suggestions concerning the poems herein enclosed. Heartfelt thanks are also due to Albert Goldbarth, Greg and Caridwen Spatz, Christine Holbert, David Luckert, Tony Flinn, and others too numerous to name, for their friendship and support. And, as always, these poems could not have been written without the love and companionship of Barbara Ellen Anderson, who has kept me from going crazy and destroying my computer.

This book is dedicated to the memory of
William Stafford, Tom Lux, Patricia Goedicke, Adam Hammer,
Madeline Defrees. Dev Hathaway, David Lenson, and Bob Abel:
wonderful writers, dear friends.
May they rest in peace and in poems.

I

For the Turn of the Year

The kind of poetry I want is my love
Who comes back with the rain.

—James Wright

BLUE CHAIR

When I sit in a blue chair beside a window and listen
to the ravens discoursing upon time again

and who owns it and where it has run on alone by that
narrow river red with spillage from the mines east of us;

and when the small glass-like frogs turn from brown to green
with that look of malicious surprise you sometimes see

on grocery clerks when it turns out you are short of cash; and
when you suddenly know the shadow bending down by the china

cabinet may well be your mother trembling as she reaches
to touch one particular tilted and delicate cup, it is easy

to consider death potentially mythological and disguised
as a screen door slamming and slamming in your dream

of that nearly forgotten and beautiful house
with its coughing furnace and light leaking in and out like a burglar

who has broken into his own rooms again; when sitting as I do
like that, it is possible to imagine coming back again

and again from death, full of love and distress, furiously calm.
And is it the soul, at last, sitting there almost alone?

POEM FOR THE TURN OF THE YEAR

Though the lilac is past its bloom,
sometimes hummingbirds
alight there, each
an offering with its own melodic
color. When they depart, longing
follows them and
what is left of my heart (perhaps
only the nectar) darts away also
like the sudden thought of something
ruby-throated
and watching with its wings.
Stillness may be the left hand
of an execution or a monument
born among the lilies
with their burden of faded blossom.

Can everything really happen, even

when the fire is cold? The fox
gone over the hill? The lamp unlit
and nowhere to be found?
Is it true we are inaccurate maps
of ourselves, gardens
surprised and helpless before the mystery
of their own design?
The hour of my life is late. A first
cricket invokes the moon
across which the flocks are flying.
Such lonely unity, this starlit migration,
and under it the few remaining angels
gowned in bright leaves and swaying
like the rest of us
on their mortal stems.

TELL ME

She said tell me again
about the rain
and I said it was hard and silver
and the trees played and played
in its great falling meadows and the grass
drank and bowed down. Each summer
morning the windows of our yellow house
delighted in the breath of it.

She said tell me
of the peaches and pears
and I said the peaches were the sun's
pink fire and pears the lop-winged moon,
pendulous and repeating
and angels sat in the branches swaying and tasting.
Cherries, lit from within, dreamed all day
of pies.

She said tell again
how you loved me then.
I said because of you violets
sprang up in the cinders of my former life and again
and again it was happiness that had no shape
but you and I.

Tell me, she said, about death
and I said we handed it back and forth
like a bowl of rubies
each of which was a story, like this one,
of what would be lost.

And she said tell me again.

PURITY

My lunch box was blue with silver
along its edge, thermos held in place
by a little gate of tin, totally low tech.
I loved it. Every day it formed a piece
of my shield against the day's terrors
served up by my classmates, and Mrs. Edmiston
who delighted in bringing me to tears
over spelling and multiplication failures
at the blackboard. Even when she smirked
at me and said, "Look at him, too scared
to even try," I could think of my lunch box,
the rock of ages, safe in the dark coat closet.
Two jelly sandwiches and a peach, like hidden
friends that would sustain me.

And when at last I struck back
at Bobby Saylor who had pantsed me once
too often on the playground
in front of everyone, including hugely
entertained Mrs. Edmiston, that beautiful blue
lunch box was my weapon at the bus stop
after school. I remember
how it rang like glory against the side
of Bobby's head and wasn't even dented!
How that night I placed it carefully
among the books and shells and souvenir
holograms, those things I knew
would not betray me, and doused the light, smiling.

I might have killed him, gone to reform school
like big Fred McIlhaney who threw rocks at cars.
What were the chances? Who knew

the cost of anything then. Even our viciousness
seemed absolutely free, anointed
somehow by our childish confusion and despair.

Still, I can see myself walking down the dirt road, swinging
that box like a piece of the sky, like all consequence
and shame lightly held, almost
cast away.

PERSONAL

1. At The Very End of Summer

In our garage apartment in Corvallis
it was so hot we stripped naked
and lay on the bed, covered in wet towels
while the frat boys next door consumed
and embraced all substance and circumstance
with the two-hundred decibel
roar of armed combat in a broom closet.

Birds sat stunned on the window sills.
Of course the noise and heat reminded us
of Vietnam (to which we were certain
I would be going), where restraints of every
kind melted, where you could watch your step
and die anyway, helping to build democratic
institutions, standing strong against the arch

enemies of freedom. Sometimes we ran
through the sprinkler
and made love on the floor. It was late
September, 1966, we had been married
three months and had no inkling our life
together
would never be that good again.

In the back rooms of honkytonks in Saigon
soldiers were lining up for their five dollar blow jobs.
In woods beyond Sweet Home, the wildcat
loggers sharpened their saws, a sound
like the laughter of demons.
I kissed the sweat of her brow. She kissed

my ears and brownish pink nipples.
As they unloaded the weekly keg
and supplementary short cases, the boys
next door sang, "We gotta get out of this place."
Meanwhile, on our cold concrete floor, arms
around each other,
all we wanted was to stay.

Do you need me to tell you
how that worked out?

2. *An Empty Barrel, Listening*

This was years later, after
she took off for Alaska
but before the divorce
waiting like a pot hole, like
a Roadway Not Improved sign
at the edge of a cliff.
I was headed through Raton Pass
toward Santa Fe
and picked up a hitchhiker
who nodded at everything I said,
but would not speak.
I drove him a hundred silent miles
until he held up his hand
and pointed and I pulled over.
He got out then leaned back in
and said, "Nothing personal."

I thought, then, he was a gift
sent to teach me to shut up,
something I had clearly failed
to learn otherwise, and I thought
kindly of him at the time
for his good intention, which must
surely have counted for something.
Later my wife came down from
the north with her new boyfriend
who dropped her off in Ft. Collins
where I met her so we could spend
four agonizing days and nights
in a motel, deciding to really split up.
Because, after all, how could
a marriage survive
what we'd been through, neither
of us knowing how time

would turn it all into ordinary trouble,
had we just stopped hashing over
the betrayals and disappointments
and waited it out.

I drove her to Denver and
watched as she climbed into his
pickup and they drove away.
I was an empty barrel, listening
to the wind, thinking this
must be the nothing
that is personal.

3. Semaphore Upon the Matter of Age

Out on the frozen pond, three birds
wobble and stand as though mystified
by the solidity beneath them.
I have had to rise early to see this,
draw on wool socks, long johns,
sweaters, muffler, mittens and boots.
The birds look distractedly in my direction.

Am I a bear, perhaps? Nearly big enough
in all these clothes. Am I hungry
for duck? It's so cold I begin to dance
and now, really alarmed, the three widgeons
leap up with a squawk and fly
twenty feet farther out on the glittering dish
of pre-dawn ice.
As I hoot and flap my arms they eye me
steadily. Even from this distance I can detect
their pity for the insane
land-bound creature who has lost all sense
of decorum. Even they can see that
no matter how hard I flap
I will never fly.

When the sun comes they decide
they've had the wrong pond
all along, and wing off over cottonwoods
on the far shore, leaving me with no audience
but daylight and the stones. Still, I stay,
for no reason, because it's good to have
no reason. Because birds aren't everything.

Because cold slows down the day
(I can almost touch it now). It's winter, at last.
And I'm still dancing.

4. Having Risen in the Half Dark of 5 A.M.

The truth of a person may be
incidental, fragmentary, lost
in the accuracy of specific spillways
and rooms. And beyond
there is the early dark
with its animals, lamps pretending
to be candles, its lonely
and unseen patches of grass.
One thing from another is never
easy as lifting an arm or cup,
never as free
as waking without thought
in what could as easily be
St. Louis as San Juan
or an unnamed planet
among the impossibly distant
stars.

Nothing holds true
but the mystery of moments, one's own
mind peeling back their husks and shells,
rocking in the wind's current,
the names of God
like plants surprised by light
on a window sill.

5. The End of the Affair

He was a kind of rage,
a fire burning its own shoes
and singing with the pain

completion makes possible
by cancelling the future.

Such abstraction was nothing
he could lean on
then, as he watched her for

that last time board the ferry,
how she turned back

once to look at him then
joined the tidal sweep
of passengers down

the car deck and into
the passageway of the private

and invisible life
that would sail from him
who stood feeling the last

vestiges of her
disengage and drift out

over the water, the crying
gulls announcing this,
the hollow rooms inside him leaning

towards it as though he himself
were nothing, his own

life only the house of her
affection, burning down as he
watched.

WAKING I DO NOT WISH LIFE TO LEAVE ME SOON

What would the window say
to the sun
were I not beside it as
day comes on?
Where would the doe browsing
on windfall pears
find herself again and look
suddenly up?
I have lived always and
at some cold edge will become
like water, one thing
that does not know
it remembers or wakes.
It is deep in me
whatever it will be without
knowing, this thing I have followed
perfectly blind almost
comfortable in the dark.
How could I not have known, and yet
I have known
the simple voice of this
bell failing toward its one word,
forever sweet soundless hum.
If it is all right, I look back
cold with the tincture of night's
complacency
and am forgiven by nothing
and walk toward it even
in happiness and sleep,
carrying myself in my arms
as though I were a child.

HE ADDRESSES THE INNER LIFE

Where is the rest of me
in relation to you?
would be my first question.
Can I reach you
with a kind of kiss or touch
or praise such as one might speak
to a god? Are you
a god there in my bones,
built of passion and grief
and refusing all advice?
Sometimes I think you are a lost
swan telling a story
to rushes and ponds and longing
to fly
like the others, if there are others.
For all I know
you are a community or a nearly
invisible liquid stillness
through which I am at times
allowed to see color become perfect
again, like the morning
in which I see myself unfrightened
and forgiven and in love
timelessly walking up a green hill
in an absence of wind with one light
shining, whispering "this
is your life, be glad."

LOOKING GLASS EDGE

In rainy light
the book I dream of
raises its face asking, purring,
its little melody of private praise
extending a green wrist, gift-like
memory of a dancer
or a dance. It doesn't care
who I am or which of me might
embody its longing to bloom
along the stringlines of what may be
only the sadness of an echo or a bell.
It does not want me
to touch the soft dark of its pagination,
its binding presumption of life
after life after life
holding on, spoken, wanting each other
as fire desires itself. It knows I would
give everything to open
and step into it, but it does not care
to wake.

THE MAN'S BEST GUESS

Along the path
and in the broken elbow postures
of the peach trees
scratching their heads
about this hard early
frost, its stiff and ferociously
chill fingers reaching into everything,
he can read all the news
that is not new. No boats

have come down from the north.
No visitors early or late
and for such a long
time now, he talks to himself.
How is he
doing? Seen anything
of the crazy old man who lives
in the abandoned quarry and subsists
on nuts and sparrows?
Seen anything of himself, slowly
shrinking into a scrim
of hobbling plywood gestures, with
accompanying pentatonic humming?

The sky hurts his eyes
with its blue glass staring.
When he looks down, the ground
reminds him of graves and grass
growing over them
so that eventually even
the names of the dead will seem
to have crawled away.

He wonders what his own
name was.

He finger-carves his best guess
on the rime frosted window
that looks out on the broken pump
and the empty yard
where there used to be angels.

ANOTHER WAKING

Sound of rain
against the window and
tar paper roof.

I had been gone
a long time
and found only what
was waiting to be found
its face beautifully
heavy and light as music
drifting over a lake.

To touch such a face
to know
its angled smile caught
in me always
and its little dance meant
everything and only
the sound of rain made
for me
the old gift of freshness
that has no mother
and only the one window
to see through
and only itself to know.

OFTEN I BEGIN WITH NOTHING

but myself around me. Dancing things.
A little music. Toy truck protruding
from a clump of grass.
Or I might ask, how have I come to this
rock with my own name
carved in its cloudy light and looking
straight at me. No wonder I feel something
like a finger on my spine. No wonder
I sometimes suspect prayer may be a long

long distance call. Or am I the holy ghost
I've heard so much about?

Will there be swans at the end of time?
I think of Odysseus on the shore, chanting
I've longed forever to return and now there's no one home.
What if I pray anyway and the swans
fold themselves like letters, all my days
undeliverable, pinioned,
and I write to the outskirts of a village or an old road
winding away, "Don't leave, stay,
was what I meant to say."

OLD BEGINNINGS AND ENDS
In memory of James Wright

The horned owl moon rises
over Ohio and looks around.
Not too much
going on here where the world
waits for the dark brotherhood of evening
to stretch its wings like some huge
secret deity of the birds

who are sleeping now,
knowing only the great oak tree murmur
of old beginnings and ends.

Soon stars will slip hesitantly out
along branches
where some thought of them has nested
all day.

And in the hills
small streams will call to the deer
that it is safe again,
that nothing else knows
they are there. Even the night
will forget to look for them
as they bend toward the cool deep
dream of water.

STANDING STILL

The moon is up in the sycamores
like a signal ensnared.
It says fall is near us now.
In tangles and reeds along the river
crickets have begun to announce
the onset of that quiet
that lets the small sounds
into themselves. I used to think evening
at this time of year was the room
in which loneliness lay down
to rest, that same place
my father entered after a long day
that did not need to be remembered
or worried or decried.

Tonight I think of him
standing in the yard, considering
perhaps his old friend the willow tree,
taken down one year in a storm, its green
tresses swaying and perfect as the girl
who became my mother
asleep as always at this hour
in the dark house, a single light
burning there
like something in the heart, whatever
that might be, illuminating just this
patch of lawn where I stand
still with him, just
the two of us.

Part II

Messengers

God,
it's Ray.
Thank you for the storm
that passed north of us and for the thought
of lime. Never have our
tomatoes been so sweet.
We taste you in them.

--Ray Amorosi

SUMMER

I.

Old man on the porch in sunlight;
in his mind lobsters loll at an edge of the sea
where there will be no singing
as the moon comes up, if it ever does
again, the lobsters think, delicately moving their spoons,
dreaming reluctantly
of days that will not come and the twisted
and beautiful underwater trees
in blossom.

II.

All alone in the breakfast room, expensive
crockery cringing but arrogant
on the plate rail and behind the glittering
leaded glass cabinet doors
with their tarnished brass fixtures longing
for the house maid's ministrations, sunlight
walks the hours slowly
across that faded Moroccan rug with a closed eye
in the middle of it.

III.

Old man on the porch in sunlight, soft
voice of a breeze
in the grass. He imagines
death as an old grey horse
bending to drink from a stream, careful
not to step on the frogs.

ELEGY FOR UNCLE GLEN

I ask the spider
how I might mourn you now
or speak out some blessing
for the old sake of your soul.
How does a spider pray
with all those legs, those eyes
watching? Before I knew you
were dead, I was green with answers
or I was the fog, stalking up hill
from the bay and the docks you worked at
forty years, and had no need
for certitudes--though I supposed I knew
all the keys and windows
and cable cars rattling toward the obvious
truth: work wears us down to shiny
thread that drifts among the benches,
bent struts and saffron, all that might be
left of the days.
If I prayed, what god would believe in you, anyway,
as I did, or as the spider,
climbing an old rose in the trash,
surely must
with so many knees to go down upon
and no soul, old soul, to claim this sorrow
as its own.

EULOGY

I imagine my father standing
in the doorway of the mortuary
thinking of his brother
single-handedly constructing houses
on leftover scraps of land
in San Francisco. Pie-shaped
slabs, cartwheel-like towers
with tiny windows, five story
parallelograms one room wide.
He built them to suit the space,
paying off whoever needed
encouragement to grant the permits,
buying overstock materials
as he could afford them, knocking off
at ten to hit the tavern and tromping
home at 1:00. All those years.
Sunday afternoons at the ball park.
Each week day an eight-hour shift
on the docks and then
back to work. What did happiness
mean to him except that every
moment was itself. Maybe
he thought of youth, playing ball
with the Helser boys; all the hard
work of living the 19th century life
of which his parents could not let go;
teasing my father endlessly
as the family worked their immense
garden, chopped endless wood
and worried their way through the
Great Depression. Work was what
work taught him, that and an

absence of complaint, since no one
and nothing was listening,
since, anyway, everything was good
right up to the day he came home
early from work, lay down to rest
and died. It was years ago.
My father now, too, has gone over
into death, smiling, as I smile
thinking how fine and tough and happy
they mostly were, how they never
would have thought to grieve
for themselves, as we seem constantly
to do, though in fact we are grieving
for the answerless new world
that labors often to no purpose
and builds mainly to augment ruin
or scare itself away
from open spaces and jerry-built
crackpot works and ways before which,
against all reason, even unto death,
the tired heart delights

SOMEONE SINGING

My father and uncle poured cement for the foundation and basement walls
of the new addition. Not enough
mud for the floor, they said, standing, shaking their heads.

It was the grey of elephants and smooth when the forms came off. My cousin
and I drew faces on it
in colored chalk. I drew an owl and a lantern and it rained.

They put a tarp over the stack of lumber, sweet smelling and so unlike the garage
which smelled of dust
and old bicycles that seemed to have wondered in there on their own.

My mother hummed as she removed strange, tiny clothing from the cedar chest.
Why did we need an extra room?
When my grandparents spoke in Danish about this, they were like the movies

or something dreamed and half sunlit under a bridge. In the background I can still
    hear
the hammering and my uncle saying, "Looks good,
just like that." Tools, a faded green Buick that had become a tractor, laundry

embracing the breeze. Chickens, cats, the next door neighbors' duck that chased
our dog and the mailman. Time like a lily that would never die.
Wind in the poplars, windows darkening toward bedtime. Someone singing. Stars.

THE OLD FARMERS SPEAK TO THE NEW

We thought you would be taller than you seem.
We thought, here are the amber voices time will send
for surety and monument to corn. We thought

here is the white horse and the black
crow-like perfection which we longed to be near
as the moon is near, scratching a midnight window,

waking us again to the happiness of lonely bodies
splashed with the old night sounds. So your departures
surprised us as the sudden disappearance of a house

suggests remorse we had forgot to name. And we are
surprised also to learn you live in deserts of a piped-in
meditation and regard, but have sown no story to account

for this and no last chance. Please notice, then, the severe
slant our mouths make as we speak of you, sadness
and anger rising up at dawn to peer at your metallic barns.

A SECRET LETTER TO THE SOUL

I am thinking again of your
immaculate depth and color,
their liveries uncontending and smaller
than I could have imagined
in the early days of our dual
singularity.

Kiss me, perhaps, or, anyway don't
wake without me
are some of my thoughts of you,
though who knows the shape
and season of your listening.
Certainly I have felt your breath
in the gold pink October grass
and in water so clear it hurts
to wonder about. Certainly you are also
a kind of ongoing message
from my own bones when they balance
between panic and contentment
like a perfectly round stone
upon moments too delicate to hold
against even the smallest wind.

Oh, you sail in
and around me, you embark
and come close.
If you were a weapon, nothing
could withstand you, but it is wrong
to think this, as it is wrong to desire
that kiss for which I go on asking.
Forgive me, driven by who
knows what loneliness or fear
I slip out
onto dark water and invite myself
into your joyful house.

FOR GERALD, A LETTER

Dear Jerry:

I think of you and when I do
I think I may not see you
again, and just afterward think that you
may not see me again
either, which is and is not the same.
We had only a few hours
together, here and there, late in life, but
I think of you anyway,
think of your Pittsburgh and your Paris
and the passionate happy sadness
of your days and the great
poems of maniacal wistfulness
and love. I think it may be there has been
no one like you and no mourning
to account for your secret joy in rhubarb
and oddly floating sticks reminding you
of Poland and Queens. I guess we're both
just making this up because of the loss
of things that are still inside us, simmering
like a forgotten stove in the cellar
where the dreams of old men are becoming
boys again while someone practices the violin
upstairs in Madam Pedemska's parlor
and she shaking her head with the hopelessness
of it and the curtains agreeing with their stillness.
I guess our souls are just becoming light
and moth-like under the lamp, someone even
stranger than we are rubbing his eyes
over a sheet of paper on which
he has written "Go with God, old friend
of much and of many"
and on which
he is about to write his name.

SARTRE

A small bird the color of cement
hops note to note beside the slaughterhouse
with its unblinking plywood windows. They say
at night sometimes the killing floor screams,
that sometimes the angel of shit and blood
reclines on the roof and scrapes his arms with shells.

It's what they say. They say no one should stand
in the tangled field next door
watching the moon ascend a little
parched song the dead might know.
They say something nearby might lift its head

from willow weeds by the scummy ditch
and invoke the art of sacrifice, the beast knowledge
glowing, intimate
and beyond grief, as it is said God must be,
though what god would require our butchering
everything

over the whole earth?
They say a small bird's note to note
moment is what we have.
And now the stars are out, they say, and the fallen
apples of October choose us and the lamps of town
light up like a lie so real it must be true.

THE DAYS: A TRIPTYCH

I.

Through sycamore leaves
waving as they do, lightly, clouds
amble the edgeless blue.
Nearby a flicker offers its knife-like cry
to the breeze
as it shimmers past.
And in the shadow of a potted plant
a spider rests, alone
as though
nothing like itself has ever lived.

II.

Sometimes, on days like this,
I close my eyes and ask the air
to wander along my collarbone, secret
and obvious, almost sleepy, sunlit
as I imagine something in me must be,
I am so warm, even in shade.
I do not care how
long I stand like this, innocence
infesting me again without
intention, so that my body may be
the idea a butterfly leaves behind,
a feather light amoral perfection
like the grass.

III.

There has been much loss,
and more will come, spawn,
no doubt, of my own ignorant
flailing. And yet, on days
like this, I stand up in myself still,
hopeless and happy, emptied of even
the loneliness of spiders and men.

RELEARNING TO PRAY

We do not turn to prayers, they stalk us,
speechless with longing
so that it is almost a betrayal to speak them.

In the dead hours
when we wake, terrified
of oblivion, its endless black sky
without stars, something
like a twisted metal angel opens its
mute throat
and silence emerges, combing
its invisible hair.

A sign, perhaps,
that surely the ultimate erasure, which we
have earned, is upon us? Was it
supposed to end
like this?
No, we say, clearly it is written, all
things shall end
in a garden of singing light, not this
night after night waking, adrift
like nothing
lost in a white cup.

But at last, out of reason and luck, one
way or another, a prayer
finds us and calls forth
its own voice.
Be with me, it says. Just that,
the words gliding out alone into
a room made entirely
of listening
and sun rising over the hills.

DEVOTION

When Robert Graves' lover threw
herself out a third story window,
he leapt after her
but not before first running down
to the next lowest floor.
Something so colossally foolish,
I cannot doubt I would have done it
myself, afraid as I am
of both loss and heights.
No doubt, too, I would have been clutching
something irredeemably incongruous
at the time, a submarine sandwich or a bolo tie;
comic Ethan Frome pratfalling
into stupidity's record book,
not even a subsequently contemplated suicide
enough to live it down.

I think this and about living things down
as I watch neighbor children
chase my cat around the yard
with a butterfly net, giant
sycamores glowering down on it all
like disgruntled gods who agree
with the Lucretian idea that our world
began in chaos
and can't see that much progress has been made
since. Which is, maybe, why the cat
escapes over the fence
leaving his pursuers milling and crestfallen
by the wheelbarrow in my driveway
where I left it this morning
after discovering how beautifully it seemed

to dwell just there, in blank defiance
of function and a long list of instructions
given me earlier concerning its employment.

Chaos again, presumably
asserting itself through me
as I left it to come in
and pour scotch into a cold Pepsi
and listen to Giuseppe DiStefano belt out
an aria from Donizetti's *L'elisir d'amore*
and look out at the foolish sunlight
leaping down photon by photon after itself
in full view of the fallen world.

FRIEND

The Psalmist said, "Lord, how shall I not
call thy name?" The hills were green with
his wonder and the birds flew filled
with singing, so he sang, "Lord, how shall I
not know thee upon the mountain
when thy sheep are the great stars of Heaven,
thy horn the sun and moon, and all the fields
bloom as thy glance approves?"

Under meditative graces of the trees, the Psalmist

sat him down without hindrance or favor.
Under his gaze rivers ran glinting among cedars
toward the dark blue paths strewn
with rushes and bordered with white stones.
And who did the Psalmist chance to see walking there
but the Lord and the Lord's loneliness, that friend
so much like ourselves
and so lost in what cannot be done about it.

HER STICKY NAME

She was only slightly darker than the others,
at first, darker as a bright day darkens
from looking at it.
She was not encrypted, desalinated,
or intravenous, not at all that
strange, simply
unexpected
like an inflatable policeman
in your grandmother's closet or a zebra
made entirely of funnels.
When she lay down, the whole world
desired her
and deflected its desire
by thinking of molten shrubberies
and crossing its legs, though the world
was surprised to discover it had legs.
Still, she enjoyed many seasons
of unrequited worship, many hats
and slow loops on the trapeze.
What she wanted tore at her fig leaves
and lips. What she disdained left town
and launched a thousand thousand
ships that sank dreaming of her shoals
as though falling toward them
from the top of an immense hen.
Day by day she grew from slightly large
to minimally huge, until she was more or less
a planet, or a room built of nothing but size,
her singing terrible for its loudness
and for our gathering around, campfire style,
making small smoky gestures of approval
and carving her sticky name, which was
forbidden us, into all our parts.

CARVED IN AIR

I.

She said, the lover mists up from an early frost
asking the time, folding
and refolding that lost and flag-like message
by which the strange captain declined his soul.

II.

Come home why don't you is my thought of **her**
who spoke and kept her numb shadow
reaching like a gaze,
who lit the black candle and passed by as I slept
for her only, my hands
a puppetry of blank pages or that barn
where absence gnaws its stall.

III.

Is it true what we love is another life, a shut **door**
that moves as we move? I walked
all the way to Pelham, once, thinking this, **knocking,**
hoping my shoes would last.

IV.

Captain of what? I wondered.

MATERIALISM

Archilochus woke among the dead
lightly sugared with Anatolian snow
and could find neither his javelin
nor shield among the cut and slouched
pieces of men full of agony and rest.

He walked unconcerned all morning
beside the death
he should have been.

When he found at last the Greek
encampment, they said, Archilochus!
We thought you were dead!
And he said, Death thought so, too.

Hills in the distance were purple and brown.
The wind was bitter. It was 655 B.C.
Archilochus sat down and ate the half raw
gobbets of roast goat, thinking, without rancor,
of his javelin and shield, chewing slowly.

NOT ALICE

It all appears so thin, so glass
and stick-like
dancing on the consolation of a blade.
Even time and the woman you loved
in it
freeze to wisps and half
forgotten splinters of sex and light.

So when she comes
back to you, you're blinded
and everything is an edge-wise marriage
between memory and one last train you're suddenly
waiting for, the midnight sorrow of its whistle
sliding toward you like a Betelguesian
lament about distance
from that place where the rail thin heart is,

where
when you go there they have to
wonder what is that shining mercy
of which you are no longer made
when, standing sideways like that,
you seem composed of something
strangely without color or cost, something
nameless and forgetting to offer itself

white-rabbit-like
but one-and-a-half dimensional, edgy: a suicide
bomber who loves his children,
a de-refinery that unmakes gasoline and puts it back
into the dreaming black lakes
of dinosaur bones.

Anyway, anyway, it's lonely where your image
wanders between the silver backing
and the glass, where reflection cannot be
what you are, where you are
only the shame or shape

of a being dreamt of
in another room and the train
declines to stop.

A MESSENGER

I heard you arrive, soft fist
against the glass sliding door,
and found you perfect
as an image of yourself on the grey
boards of the porch,
eyes still fixed on the shining
sheet of sky that killed you.
No name, really, comes with this
sadness. The rust of things, their fracture
and falling away like moments, or
those angels we wish for and never see.
Your silk soft russet and black breast is warm
still, as though you might suddenly stand
and fly up into the fiery maple again.
But you are in the underlife where my child, the one
who could not fly and was lost,
has been these many years.
I hope you will tell her I handed you
gently into the tall grass behind the house,
that I grieved for you and all mortal accident, that I know
she has the heart of a beautiful bird, now,
somewhere in time or its absence,
that I blew on you softly in case you might be brought
to breathe again.

NIGHT TIME

Though it was dark and the curtains
drawn, I could feel the snow
in fields behind the house
and the wind asking to come in.
Awake in my bed by a small window
I imagined the moon out beyond the orchard
trying to speak
or flutter one of its tourmaline eyes
at our scarecrow
slow dancing on his stick, miming crucifixion
or possibly waving goodbye.
If time was passing, it did not want
anyone to know. It seemed
everything slept but me, nine years old,
sharing a room with my brother
who was three and blond and deep
in his dreaming happiness.
I wondered, as I wondered every night,
what huge silent song bird
would visit me, grooming
its silver beak and laying open the roof
to stars that night after night asked
who was I, really, drifting through space
in the dark? Maybe
I counted to a thousand, breathing in
planets and trees and the shadowy insistence
of everything that wasn't there.
Maybe my parents lolled in the vast
prairie of the next room like all odd
beasts, suffused with distance
and exhaustion.
God was nearby, too, inside my thumbnail

saying his prayers
in which I was not mentioned, though, also,
disguised as a chair, he sat in the dark
beside me
quietly counting the hours
and keeping them, so that if by chance sleep
found me, I should not wake
and be afraid

III

The Godly Sea

And then went down to the ship,
Set keel to breakers, forth on the godly sea, and
We set up mast and sail on that swart ship,
Bore sheep aboard her, and our bodies also
Heavy with weeping, and winds from sternward
Bore us out onward with bellying canvas...,

--Ezra Pound

THE GODLY SEA

1. Low Tide

Grey rock, mud flats, and a few crabs,
my axe glinting through summer light
in which the great
heron stands like a snag of glass, a beautifully bent
arrow in a window frame.

*   *   *

Any minute I will fill my lungs
with the new day
as I go down the ivy-tangled path to look
among sea wrack and the rocks
to see has tide left me more wood or a curious scrap
of some forgotten thing. Thirty-six

years ago.
It is immensely quiet. The old elk hound, Haakon,
labors through brambles
to be near me.
As the wind freshens, we sit and place
our chins upon our paws.

2. Night Ops

I walked along the dim
passageway after lights out
while three decks up
the boom and slap of night
launch and recovery ops
carried on under the calm
north Atlantic starlight.
There were no
emergencies. The Marines
had finally quit polishing
their weapons and boots
and turned in exactly
as ordered. The recruits
on the mess decks had survived
their eighteen hour
purgatory and straggled off
to their sweltering
compartment. I was thinking
about moonlit Hawthorn Street
as it ran under the roof-like
boughs of maples lining it
between 82nd and 89th
so that a boy might walk
and feel himself alone there,
true or not, and might be
remembering the glow
of his girl's skin
as she leaned back
to kiss him again and
again until the hours
deserted them and they
did things that made him

dizzy with happiness
even then, having gone off
to war, having become what
boys become and found himself,
in the enclosed twi-night
of that ship, become myself
thinking of us both, as I am
doing now, and of that girl
and Hawthorn Street
in the warm embracing dark
in which not much was known
or feared
and each moment opened
like a rose
or the wings of night hawks
circling above the streetlamps
as though looking, like memory,
for home
or the perfect place to land.

3. The Four Directions

*"You divide yourself and witness yourself
and it makes no difference."* Larry Levis

You watch the ferry arrive
and consider that, in another
simultaneous life, you might be

on it, staring out toward this
window with a man behind it
thinking of you as though

you were himself, which
may be the case, but you don't
know.

Or you may be
the man in the dinghy dead
in the path of the ferry

and rowing as though possessed,
furious at the two men like yourself
staring at you, fused

somehow to the question of whether
you will live or be chopped up
in the ferry's enormous screws.

A fourth man, in a sail boat anchored
nearby, believes the rest of you insane.
But, though none of this has happened,

the truth of it goes on by itself, even
supposing no one is there
to affirm an absence of the actual,

though absence itself would, naturally,
be invisible. And so perhaps everything
is unseen

supposition, you and I
and all of us
waiting to appear, waving and jolly,

counting ourselves luckily
possible, no matter who or when
or what we might have been,

or who might have written this,
wildly exultant in his joyous disbelief
and sadness.

4. Bread Upon the Waters

*Cast thy bread upon the waters: for thou
shalt find it again after many days.*

Ecclesiastes 11:1

Under a pile of documents, old books
and clothes of no use to anyone,
I found my father's casting reel,
still snug in its velvet bag inside
the box it came in, its perfect
chrome crank and spindle
gleaming like treasure uncovered
in an Egyptian tomb. It cost him
almost more money than he had.
And then for decades
up to his neck in children and work
he barely touched it
so that it became a promise: someday,
maybe a little twelve-foot runabout
and a one-room place by a small lake
with trout. Someday, if everything broke
just right, which everything seemed
disinclined to do. The Bill of Rights,
Hammurabi's Code, English Common
Law, nothing protected a man's luck.
But when it was almost sundown
he managed to buy the boat, retrieved
the reel from its box and for his last
years, when the weather was fine,
cruised forth upon the nearby lakes
and rivers with a kind of peaceful
gratitude and caught nothing, mostly,
but shimmering and illusive time,
and returned home with it as though
that were the real prize.

5. The Sea Side
       after Alberto Rios

The old women look a little
like men
and the men look
a little like November's petunias.

It is long ago
already.

One of the flower-like men
thinks of a glass
globe he held up to the light
as a child, everything
inside perfect;
and on the tiny streets and houses,
on the men and women there
in their strange, elaborate clothes,
snow was falling.

Something invisible in a corner (perhaps
it is myself) observes
the papery light and scent
of lavender
where the women sit
looking a little like stories that have become
curious
and afraid that any breeze might
wake them in a country of abandoned
parasols and high lace shoes.

They know the Devil
is ignoring them now, that the men

are waving their arms at nothing.
No one thinks of or speaks about
the sea. No one is in harness
anymore.
And the days themselves are like a story
made of those ancient agreements
concerning time's profligate
determinacy, without the sex part,

made with virtually no
materials
but a step by step unfolding
and the beauty of it, though everyone knows
it will end beside the sea no one
(not even I, who have brought them here)
will recognize or remember.

6. At Quartermaster Harbor, 1986

The Harvest Moon rose fireball orange,
striking a path
through which one lonely skiff
rowed, oar locks thumping a bit
with the irregular pull of its occupant.
Dangerous out there in the dark
for a small, flat-bottomed craft
without even a nine-horse outboard
to keep it from harm.

A heron squawked as its huge silhouette
rose from the shallows
and rowed across the moon like an example
of how it should be done.

On a stump above the harbor, the old
dog asleep at our feet, she and I
sat, watching. She was five
years old. The memory is like
a recurring dream that will not stay
focused or a doorless room I long to enter.
It is as though if something
weren't missing in me, I could go there
and all the terrible past would be undone

and death would have no dominion
and the skiff would arrive safely
on the other shore.

7. Another Theory of the Afterlife

After death the days will be enormous
gardens with poppies and flamingos
and light making everything ripple
in the eternal placidity of being.
Cold streams will invite the boat-like soul
to lean back in them and drift
and never trouble again about time
or infamy, regardless of whatever strange
shore may be glimpsed in passing.

8. Ship of Old Men

We cast off as though
giving all we had to luck, ignoring
the clouds and spiral motions
of the terns and starlings, the frigid
breath of the mountain behind us.

The houses of our lives backed
into their shadows
as we turned to the changeling mysteries
of water, ever receding from our loves
constructed plank by ancient wish and dare,
the voices of spray and wind
replacing it all.

Oh, I suppose
it was grief we wanted, a thorn to prove
that we had lived,
in spite of the obvious folly of this.

I remember thinking of Tennyson's
Ulysses as he intoned,
It may be we shall touch the Happy Isles
And see the great Achilles, whom we knew...,
thinking of him bound out, pure hazard
balanced by the wonder of his nerve
to set aside all but this single

integrated act. Likewise, as an arrow
become, classically, its own target,
we gathered and set forth,
tightened sail and thought calmly
of all we had lost and won
and lost, final and bound out
upon "the godly sea."

Part IV

Come Near Us Again

Now I carry those days in a tiny box
Wherever I go. I open the lid like this
And let the light glimpse and then glance away.
There is a sigh like my breath when I do this.
Some days I do this again and again.

—*William Stafford*

A CONTINGENCY

In the dream of the old shoemaker, Edgar Allan Poe
is crossing an Inca bridge
blindfolded, a little high, perhaps for once literally.

A thousand feet below, water white as the jaguar's tooth
roars as though hungry.
The half-rotted planks of the bridge buckle and sway

and Poe smiles with terrified appreciation, counting each
step as death defeated
one more time and celebrated by a harsh tonic note

in the heavens and all through the rock-strewn altiplano
where the shoemaker
finds suddenly himself, seated before a glowing and enormous

cobbler's last, hammering Poe's face into a ballet slipper
with a small moustache.
"God be praised," he says, in case this is neither his dream

nor someone else's.

EACH NIGHT AN OPERA HOUSE

I.

Nijinsky wakes up in the grave
and does a little pearl-like dance
for the amusement of the great crystal spider
that claps and claps like a galaxy
calling its children home.

Some kind of tide
brushes the face of his uniform
and the footlights come up.
He dances deliberately quiet
as a lake somewhere wishing all of Paris
awake again, dumbfounded
by the alien bloom of his body turned
to music, a kind of lonely happiness
frightening a room, its arms
becoming wings again
joining the dead swans in their millions.

Each night is an opera house
no one knew was there. Centuries
step away from the wall and Nijinsky
embraces them as if what lives there were
a kind of forgetting
reborn with each
elegant leap into the darkening air.

II.

Is this a homecoming, his twirling
grey garments answering a whistle

like the doomed legions
who will go "over the top" in that war
that will rage and rage
and end, finally, nothing but itself?
Impossibly again among the vanished
crowds and their cheering, he begins
to consider his descent. Will he
lilt down like a leaf?
Topple like a tower thrown down
by a giant's mad despair?
As always, much is unexplained.

For instance, dreaming this
exactly,
we might wonder if we, the earthbound,
do not also have the right to spring,
so to speak,
even as we wonder at his sailing,
arms outstretched as if to grasp
in mid-air a dreamed kingdom
between love that has broken down
and a Heaven that, though empty,
may still be there.

NOAH AT LAST

He walks like a man waking
to find himself
cured and whistling,

young again.

Frost twinkles on the path
his steps create.
Swans blaze like moonlight

on the slow stream. Death says,

this way to the finish line,
and maybe so. Regardless, the man
keeps walking

west. All this time

he has been nothing
but a destination, ticking,
whittling,

missing

the great migrations,
salt of the earth so briefly
all there is.

Day darkens and Death sits at his right hand

writing it all down, the man
coming home at twilight as though
it were possible,

as though he and Death had forgotten

the word that names them both
and the rules of the game
they have been at

so long. In this arrival,

the beautiful light of existence
invents itself
and goes away without them

like a kind of singing found

without the usual
terror worrying
again what may matter

to them or God and what may not.

Oh, the peaceful starlight
full of creatures and the man
almost sailing among them

like a promise no one remembers.

Home, he says, closing his eyes, thinking
of a black dove
placing an olive sprig

on his shoulder.

FLOOD

I.

Even in our sleep we hear it, the roar of everything
and nothing much
passing over us like Fortune and Justice drunk
laughing it up in the bar next door, pig iron loads
of unanswerable prayer and imprecation
stuck to their large old shoes.

II.

Caution! Stay Where You Are! Please Leave
Your Payment in the Blood Red Cup.

Dear son, come home, we've decided to spare the dog
and hang you.

One step at a time now. You can make it. The water
is not that deep.

III.

We're out of sugar and we're out of light. Someone
keeps saying there is a giant assigned to each of us,
that you can hear them wading, seeking us out
in our nailed shut rooms below the stairs.

One of the giants keeps saying he loves us all, he really does.
And the others trust him, see, though he's nothing
but a whisper in the hard dark
beside us,

though he's a woman, too, or the mink soft touch
of an accident or a moon we didn't know was there
all along, shining
as though nothing in the world were wrong.

LIVING ALONE

I.

In the time of the day lilies blooming
and the dusky smoke of peat
a man rises like a shirt full of wind.

He has been all night unloading the witch hazel
of a moment in which he was again a soldier
or a phrase in the soldier's last letter:

Dear Amelia, memory tells me of our hands
all night crossing
our own river, widening
the tongues of its shelter intertwined.
A kindness amid all this murder.

II.

Candle in a window. Something silver
and a chill rain chiming
on the sill. So much
to remember, stepping out again
onto the grass: oiling the soldier's rifle,
finding again his prayers drifting up
beyond all rain
into starlit years of paper and shells.
Who was it lived in the calm, worn penny
of that face?
His body barely worth itself, is he nothing
but a garment now, an old pair of wings
in a shed?

Nevertheless, he stands in the dark
and whistles, "Here I am
temporary, bird-like and eternal inhabitant
of a stranger's house, his objects and hours,
his flags of surrender, the hermetic
meaning of every threadbare thing
he meant to be."

III.

It isn't really death that talks
this way. It is the shadow of what
cannot be said always
straining to materialize
and the man astonished
to find he must think of existence
to fully exist; and in his thought finding
himself alone with the sound of a key
in the lock, and not knowing
whether he is out or in or is
perhaps himself the key
in something's pocket, singing
a little song.

MEMORY'S HOUSE

The back door bangs
against the house.
Through what were once windows
jagged light leaks
onto chewed up chairs and curtains.
Whatever's nesting in the corners
should probably be left alone.
Go ahead and be the telephone
ringing somewhere out of reach.
Whoever might be seeking you
cannot be a friend and anyway
the damp cellar wonders
who would call, who would
climb the stair of missing steps
and pace the hall, enter that door
where all the lights are out
and the moon
is a mess on the floor.

WHAT HAS BECOME

The cloudy look of a Cezanne landscape
suggests a figure will shortly
emerge from the trees, straightening
his hat
which will be dark as almost all
the rest of him, except
the face leaking a flesh-colored light,
and the one raised hand
that is a kind of flag
or perhaps a bit of semaphore
if you squint.
It might be supposed
he is on his way to the village
for bread or wine, or to meet
secretly with Madam Suchet
whose husband is away in Paris
on business. On his way
he may incidentally encounter
"The Bathers" disporting themselves
in a path-side pond.

We cannot see clearly his high laced
shoes, the strangely formal
pattern formed by the buttons on his coat.
But we perceive no malice
in his posture
or his step. We think
his name may be Armand, owner
of a stationer's shop, presently
tended—as is often the case—by his wife,
Genevieve, who is pregnant again.

He will, we are certain, not be long
away, since he carries no luggage.
And so, unless run down by a carriage or
arrested for criminal
conversation, he will walk back in among
shadows of the painted trees, eventually.
We must admit, however, the chance
that upon the occasion of his return
from his possible appearance there,
he will turn too sharply
at a critical
juncture (a dropped brush, perhaps)
and find himself
in a loud and terrible world no one
could ever have wanted, where huge
machines roar above and upon the land
and the air is bitter with human hurry
and disgust.

Breathless with the force of it, perhaps
he rests his head against a pile of stones, thinking
what
has become of the beautiful world?
Even Cezanne, standing a hundred and twenty
years, brush poised
above a canvas that has begun
to trouble him, might well struggle
to remember it.

SOME WARS NEVER END

It is a long way down a gun barrel
to where the children die
in their party-colored clothes.
You can barely hear their cries,
so much like joy

you want to toss something in the air
along with your tears.
You want to go home a long time.
You offer your legs, your arms
if only the children might be spared.

You want to go home, even without
arms, to hold them again, without luck
or anything that could crawl back
miraculously alive as a smile
or an old man waking from this dream

to wonder where have they all gone
and who were those grey men who screamed
and screamed as though they were angry
or afraid.

LAMONT CRANSTON IN RETIREMENT

I'm up late in the lemon-like light
of a lamp
among the ghostly absences leaking
from photographs and books.
Here we are again, they whisper,
at thy right hand, so to speak, the hand
you're using now, scratching away, leaving
your ridiculous marks.

It's their usual choral address, giving form
to a sarcastic disappointment
in the life they do not have.
Or maybe it's teasing.
Who can tell with the dead and inanimate?
The Shadow knows, I say, nostalgically
entertained but lonely for the blind power
of Radio again.

"Circularity," I murmur, "strobe light," "fog,"
just for something to say,
and pretend their amazement
as I hold out to them pinks and lilies
that have followed me home from a vision
of ancient gardens and upon which my mind
has drawn tiny faces and hands.

I lived all my fictive life alone, and so
do not know but suppose everyone must do this
kind of thing, late at night, in some way
consoling the need to shape themselves
in the face of loss
and loss, to acknowledge an illusive perfection,

as if suddenly remembering the name
of a color made of music
or wind.

Nevertheless everyone
must also go on wondering why (really)
stay up like this, as though we ourselves
were the ghosts, as though
these dark hours and whispers were the actual
and nameless life and everything else
the dream of it, insubstantial as a shape
in black hat and cape, laughing
as it melts through a wall.

THE HERO'S DREAM OF THE END OF THE WORLD

I.

I lit the fire and the lamp. Dark
edged away from the room.
surprise!
I said
to a bowl on a shelf above the sink.
I'll bet you thought I was alone
with darkness all
around and the little bit
of wind.
Mercy, I said, is little
and cold; sometimes you
even hear its touch
on your arm.
Sometimes it walks right
out on you
and leaves the door to the vestry
or the sty
hanging by one hinge.

II.

What made me say that
was the thought of music
and time's pointless
metronomic passion, like frantic
swimming
after the ship has gone down, sharks
everywhere, imaginary lights.
You've probably heard this
but most mornings I cast
no shadow

to speak of, and no voice
to see. I am a rose
in a lightless room, windows
painted over with an absence of birds.
You probably think I'm asleep
again, curled up tight
to my wishes and getting it
wrong.
Sue me; the truth
is a mirror
behind you on the wall.

III.

A boat way off
in the channel says its one
syllable. Somewhere nearby
an owl is asking.
Don't let me keep you, I think love
is walking up my spine
in very small shoes,
in a snow
of blossoms I don't deserve.
So that's something.
But what could anyone deserve?
Morning and the grey
progress toward dawn. Can I
have meant a word of this?
God steps out of that question
holding a sign. What if it said,
"No worries, Pillar of Salt.
I have turned back toward the fire
also,
waiting for you."

THE MAGICIAN IS SURPRISED TO FIND
NOTHING IN HIS HAT

There is nothing up my sleeve
or hidden in my hair,
except a low hanging bit
of sky-blue winter, which
is what happens
at our age or ageless
ness, as may be, turning
in a light wind
or swimming in a kind of style
flattened by prayer or use.
This is a truth I
once told you, lying
in spring's creamery and silk,
a kind of heaven without
the angels, dear angel, and now
we have only the past
for wings.
Did we actually hear the singing?
Forgive me, I have to ask—
it is that lonely now, lonely
as a whisper
carried up hill in the dark as if
by slight-of-hand and without
either of us.

GHOST TO GHOST

I've called you back to me
because why not, both of us
alone, sunk in distance and the harm of it?
Dry leaves, dizzying down in separate forests
somewhere, do not have our options.
So why don't you die
out of the shadow life, return, as I have,
with nothing, not even your old face
emptied of memory's black and blue
devotions. All day I whisper

of the body's new covenant emerging
like leaves that will never fall in this
revised kingdom where you will find me
dancing.

I know none of this
makes the kind of happiness we dare not
keep alive. I know rapprochement
is pentimento to original loss, an empty boat
spinning a little in the rain and sun
of time's declined complexities.
It's abstract, I know,
when I talk about it. Just
forget it all. Come back to me, begin
to choose another life.

ABOVE THE OAKS PARK AMUSEMENT ARCADE
THE BELOVED DEAD COME NEAR US AGAIN
—for Lori Beth Howell Bond, in memoriam

Above the river and the skating rink lights
gone out, the dead gather
again, and wish I would shut up
and listen. And no touching, they say,
no bright day returning.
All they want is the dusty shine
they have become, and that I stop longing
for their empty shells
and simply take one step nearer the chilled

ahistorical flame of their actuality,
their timelessness that is like water, or
a memory with nothing in it.

Turn your head slightly away and see us,
they say, we are love's night vision, the hearing
that whispers up your arms. Here
beyond nobility and chance, we are perfect
and close.
To know us again, think of lights
on the river of the mind, the barkers calling
everyone, even the beloved, who have left
no forwarding address, back for one more ride.

Born in Portland, Oregon, Christopher Howell attended Pacific Lutheran and Oregon State Universities, and, after serving as a military journalist during the Viet Nam war, received graduate degrees from Portland State University and the University of Massachusetts. He is author of twelve previous collections of poems, most recently *The Grief of a Happy Life* (U. Washington Press, 2019), *Love's Last Number* and *Gaze* (both from Milkweed Editions), and *Dreamless and Possible: Poems New and Selected* (U. Washington Press, 2010). He has received the Washington State Governor's Award, the Washington State Book Award, two fellowships from National Endowment for the Arts, two from the Artist Trust, and a number of other fellowships and awards, including three Pushcart prizes. His poems, essays, and interviews may be found in many journals and in more than forty-five anthologies. Since 1996 he has lived in Spokane, where he is Emeritus Professor on Eastern Washington University's Master of Fine Arts in Creative Writing faculty. He is married to the artist Barbara Ellen Anderson, and they have a son, Evan, who is also a painter.

CPSIA information can be obtained
at www.ICGtesting.com
Printed in the USA
LVHW041507210722
723437LV00002B/11

9 781622 882335